On the Creed

On the Creed

St. Augustine

On the Creed

© Lighthouse Publishing 2018

Written by: St. Augustine (Nov.13 354 – Aug.28 430)

Translated by: Rev. C. L. Cornish. M.A.

Updated into Modern U.S English by A.M. Overett (b. 1960)

All rights reserved. Without limiting the rights under copyright reserved above, no part of this publication may be reproduced, stored in a retrieval system, or transmitted, in any form or by any means (electronic, mechanical, photocopying, recording or otherwise), without the prior written permission of the copyright owner of this book.

Published by
Lighthouse Christian Publishing
SAN 257-4330
5531 Dufferin Drive
Savage, Minnesota, 55378
United States of America

www.lighthousechristianpublishing.com

1. Receive, my children, the Rule of Faith, which is called the Symbol (or Creed). And when ye have received it, write it in your heart, and be daily saying it to yourselves; before ye sleep, before ye go forth, arm you with your Creed. The Creed no man writes so as it may be able to be read: but for rehearsal of it, lest haply forgetfulness obliterate what care hath delivered, let your memory be your record-roll: what ye are about to hear, that are ye to believe; and what ye shall have believed, that are about to give back with your tongue. For the Apostle says, "With the heart man believeth unto righteousness, and with the mouth confession is made unto salvation." For this is the Creed which ye are to rehearse and to repeat in answer. These words which ye have heard are in the Divine Scriptures scattered up and down: but thence gathered and reduced into one, that the memory of slow persons might not be distressed; that every person may be able to say, able to hold, what he believes. For have ye now merely heard that God is Almighty? But ye begin to have him for your father, when ye have been born by the church as your Mother.

2. Of this, then, ye have now received, have meditated, and having meditated have held, that ye should say, "I believe in God the Father Almighty." God is Almighty, and yet, though Almighty, He cannot die, cannot be deceived, cannot lie; and, as the Apostle says, "cannot deny Himself." How many things that He cannot do, and yet is Almighty! yea therefore is Almighty, because He cannot do these things. For if He could die, He were not Almighty; if to lie, if to be deceived, if to do unjustly, were possible for Him, He were not Almighty: because if this were in Him, He should not be worthy to

be Almighty. To our Almighty Father, it is quite impossible to sin. He does whatsoever He will: that is Omnipotence. He does whatsoever He rightly will, whatsoever He justly will: but whatsoever is evil to do, He wills not. There is no resisting one who is Almighty, that He should not do what He will. It was He Who made heaven and earth, the sea, and all that in them is, invisible and visible. Invisible such as are in heaven, thrones, dominions, principalities, powers, archangels, angels: all, if we shall live aright, our fellow-citizens. He made in heaven the things visible; the sun, the moon, the stars. With its terrestrial animals He adorned the earth, filled the air with things that fly, the land with them that walk and creep, the sea with them that swim: all He filled with their own proper creatures. He made also man after His own image and likeness, in the mind: for in that is the image of God. This is the reason why the mind cannot be comprehended even by itself, because in it is the image of God. To this end were we made, that over the other creatures we should bear rule: but through sin in the first man we fell, and are all come into an inheritance of death. We were brought low, became mortal, were filled with fears, with errors: this by desert of sin: with which desert and guilt is every man born. This is the reason why, as ye have seen to-day, as ye know, even little children undergo exsufflation, exorcism; to drive away from them the power of the devil their enemy, which deceived man that it might possess mankind. It is not then the creature of God that in infants undergoes exorcism or exsufflation: but he under whom are all that are born with sin; for he is the first of sinners. And for this cause by reason of one who fell and brought all into death, there was sent One without sin, Who should bring unto life, by delivering them from sin, all that believe on Him.

3. For this reason we believe also in His Son, that is to say, God the Father Almighty's, "His Only Son, our Lord." When thou hears of the Only Son of God, acknowledge Him God. For it could not be that God's Only Son should not be God. What He is, the same did He beget, though He is not that Person Whom He begot. If He be truly Son, He is that which the Father is; if He be not that which the Father is, He is not truly Son. Observe mortal and earthly creatures: what each is, that it engendered. Man besets not an ox, sheep besets not dog, nor dog sheep. Whatever it be that begets, that which it is, it begets. Hold ye therefore boldly, firmly, faithfully, that the Begotten of God the Father is what Himself is, Almighty. These mortal creatures engender by corruption. Does God so beget? He that is begotten mortal generates that which himself is; the Immortal generates what He is: corruptible begets corruptible, Incorruptible begets Incorruptible: the corruptible begets corruptibly, Incorruptible, Incorruptibly: yea, so begets what Itself is, that One begets One, and therefore Only. Ye know, that when I pronounced to you the Creed, so I said, and so ye are bounden to believe; that we "believe in God the Father Almighty, and in Jesus Christ His Only Son." Here too, when thou believes that He is the Only, believe Him Almighty: for it is not to be thought that God the Father does what He will, and God the Son does not what He will. One Will of Father and Son, because one Nature. For it is impossible for the will of the Son to be any whit parted from the Father's will. God and God; both one God: Almighty and Almighty; both One Almighty.

4. We do not bring in two Gods as some do, who say, "God the Father and God the Son, but greater God the Father and lesser God the Son." They both are what? Two Gods? Thou blushes to speak it, blush to believe it. Lord God the Father, thou says, and Lord God the Son: and the Son Himself says, "No man can serve two Lords." In His family shall we be in such wise, that, like as in a great house where there is the father of a family and he hath a son, so we should say, the greater Lord, the lesser Lord? Shrink from such a thought. If ye make to yourselves such like in your heart, ye set up idols in the "one soul." Utterly repel it. First believe, then understand. Now to whom God gives that when he has believed he soon understands; that is God's gift, not human frailness. Still, if ye do not yet understand, believe: One God the Father, God Christ the Son of God. Both are what? One God. And how are both said to be One God? How? Does thou marvel? In the Acts of the Apostles, "There was," it says, "in the believers, one soul and one heart." There were many souls, faith had made them one. So many thousands of souls were there; they loved each other, and many are one: they loved God in the fire of charity, and from being many they are come to the oneness of beauty. If all those many souls the dearness of love made one soul, what must be the dearness of love in God, where is no diversity, but entire equality! If on earth and among men there could be so great charity as of so many souls to make one soul, where Father from Son, Son from Father, hath been ever inseparable, could They both be other than One God? Only, those souls might be called both many souls and one soul; but God, in Whom is ineffable and highest conjunction, may be called One God, not two Gods.

5. The Father doeth what He will, and what He will doeth the Son. Do not imagine an Almighty Father and a not Almighty Son: it is error, blot it out within you, let it not cleave in your memory, let it not be drunk into your faith, and if haply any of you shall have drunk it in, let him vomit it up. Almighty is the Father, Almighty the Son. If Almighty begat not Almighty, He begat not very Son. For what say we, brethren, if the Father being greater begat a Son less than He? What said I, begat? Man engenders, being greater, a son being less: it is true: but that is because the one grows old, the other grows up, and by very growing attains to the form of his father. The Son of God, if He grows not because neither can God wax old, was begotten perfect. And being begotten perfect, if He grows not, and remained not less, He is equal. For that ye may know Almighty begotten of Almighty, hear Him Who is Truth. That which of Itself Truth says, is true. What says Truth? What says the Son, Who is Truth? "Whatsoever things the Father doeth, these also the Son likewise doeth." The Son is Almighty, in doing all things that He wills to do. For if the Father doeth some things which the Son doeth not, the Son said falsely, "Whatsoever things the Father doeth, these also the Son doeth likewise." But because the Son spoke truly, believe it: "Whatsoever things the Father doeth, these also the Son doeth likewise," and ye have believed in the Son that He is Almighty. Which word although ye said not in the Creed, yet this is it that ye expressed when ye believed in the Only Son, Himself God. Hath the Father aught that the Son hath not? This Arian heretic blasphemers say, not I. But what say I? If the Father hath aught that the Son hath not, the Son lies in saying, "All things that the Father hath, are Mine." Many and innumerable are the

testimonies by which it is proved that the Son is Very Son of God the Father, and the Father God hath His Very-begotten Son God, and Father and Son is One God.

6. But this Only Son of God, the Father Almighty, let us see what He did for us, what He suffered for us. "Born of the Holy Ghost and of the Virgin Mary." He, so great God, equal with the Father, born of the Holy Ghost and of the Virgin Mary, born lowly, that thereby He might heal the proud. Man exalted himself and fell; God humbled Himself and raised him up. Christ's lowliness, what is it? God hath stretched out a hand to man laid low. We fell, He descended: we lay low, He stooped. Let us lay hold and rise, that we fall not into punishment. So then His stooping to us is this, "Born of the Holy Ghost and of the Virgin Mary." His very Nativity too as man, it is lowly, and it is lofty. Whence lowly? That as man He was born of men. Whence lofty? That He was born of a virgin. A virgin conceived, a virgin bore, and after the birth was a virgin still.

7. What next? "Suffered under Pontius Pilate." He was in office as governor and was the judge, this same Pontius Pilate, what time as Christ suffered. In the name of the judge there is a mark of the times, when He suffered under Pontius Pilate: when He suffered, "was crucified, dead, and buried." Who? what? for whom? Who? God's Only Son, our Lord. What? Crucified, dead, and buried. For whom? for ungodly and sinners. Great condescension, great grace! "What shall I render unto the Lord for all that He hath bestowed on me?"

8. He was begotten before all times, before all worlds. "Begotten before." Before what, He in Whom is no before? Do not in the least imagine any time before that Nativity of Christ whereby He was begotten of the Father; of that Nativity I am speaking by which He is Son of God Almighty, His Only Son our Lord; of that am I first speaking. Do not imagine in this Nativity a beginning of time; do not imagine any space of eternity in which the Father was and the Son was not. Since when the Father was, since then the Son. And what is that "since," where is no beginning? Therefore ever Father without beginning, ever Son without beginning. And how, thou wilt say, was He begotten, if He have no beginning? Of eternal, coeternal. At no time was the Father, and the Son not, and yet Son of Father was begotten. Whence is any manner of similitude to be had? We are among things of earth, we are in the visible creature. Let the earth give me a similitude: it gives none. Let the element of the waters give me some similitude: it hath not whereof to give. Some animal give me a similitude: neither can this do it. An animal indeed engenders, both what engenders and what is engendered: but first is the father, and then is born the son. Let us find the coeval and imagine it coeternal. If we shall be able to find a father coeval with his son, and son coeval with his father, let us believe God the Father coeval with His Son, and God the Son coeternal with His Father. On earth we can find some coeval, we cannot find any coeternal. Let us stretch the coeval and imagine it coeternal. Someone, it may be, will put you on the stretch, by saying, "When is it possible for a father to be found coeval with his son, or son coeval with his father? That the father may beget he goes before in age; that the son may be begotten, he comes after in age: but this father

coeval with son, or son with father, how can it be?" Imagine to yourselves fire as father, its shining as son; see, we have found the coevals. From the instant that the fire begins to be, that instant it begets the shining: neither fire before shining, nor shining after fire. And if we ask, which begets which? the fire the shining, or the shining the fire? Immediately ye conceive by natural sense, by the innate wit of your minds ye all cry out, The fire the shining, not the shining the fire. Lo, here you have a father beginning; lo, a son at the same time, neither going before nor coming after. Lo, here then is a father beginning, lo, a son at the same time beginning. If I have shown you a father beginning, and a son at the same time beginning, believe the Father not beginning, and with Him the Son not beginning either; the one eternal, the other coeternal. If ye get on with your learning, ye understand: take pains to get on. The being born, ye have; but also the growing, ye ought to have; because no man begins with being perfect. As for the Son of God, indeed, He could be born perfect, because He was begotten without time, coeternal with the Father, long before all things, not in age, but in eternity. He then was begotten coeternal, of which generation the Prophet said, "His generation who shall declare?" begotten of the Father without time, He was born of the Virgin in the fullness of times. This nativity had times going before it. In opportunity of time, when He would, when He knew, then was He born: for He was not born without His will. None of us is born because he will, and none of us dies when he will: He, when He would, was born; when He would, He died: how He would, He was born of a Virgin: how He would, He died; on the cross. Whatever He would, He did: because He was in such wise Man that, unseen, He was God; God assuming, Man assumed; One Christ, God and Man.

9. Of His cross what shall I speak, what say? This extreme kind of death He chose, that not any kind of death might make His Martyrs afraid. The doctrine He shewed in His life as Man, the example of patience He demonstrated in His Cross. There, you have the work, that He was crucified; example of the work, the Cross; reward of the work, Resurrection. He shewed us in the Cross what we ought to endure, He shewed in the Resurrection what we have to hope. Just like a consummate task-master in the matches of the arena, He said, Do, and bear; do the work and receive the prize; strive in the match and thou shall be crowned. What is the work? Obedience. What the prize? Resurrection without death. Why did I add, "without death?" Because "Lazarus rose, and died: Christ rose again, "dies no more, death will no longer have dominion over Him."

10. Scripture says, "Ye have heard of the patience of Job, and have seen the end of the Lord." When we read what great trials Job endured, it makes one shudder, it makes one shrink, it makes one quake. And what did he receive? The double of what he had lost. Let not a man therefore with an eye to temporal rewards be willing to have patience, and say to himself, "Let me endure loss, God will give me back sons twice as many; Job received double of all, and begat as many sons as he had buried." Then is this not the double? Yes, precisely the double, because the former sons still lived. Let none say, "Let me bear evils, and God will repay me as He repaid Job:" that it be now no longer patience but avarice. For if it was not

patience which that Saint had, nor a brave enduring of all that came upon him; the testimony which the Lord gave, whence should he have it? "Hast thou observed," says the Lord, "my servant Job? For there is not like him any on the earth, a man without fault, true worshipper of God." What a testimony, my brethren, did this holy man deserve of the Lord! And yet him a bad woman sought by her persuasion to deceive, she too representing that serpent, who, like as in Paradise he deceived the man whom God first made, so likewise here by suggesting blasphemy thought to be able to deceive a man who pleased God. What things he suffered, my brethren! Who can have so much to suffer in his estate, his house, his sons, his flesh, yea in his very wife who was left to be his tempter! But even her who was left, the devil would have taken away long ago, but that he kept her to be his helper: because by Eve he had mastered the first man, therefore had he kept an Eve. What things, then, he suffered! He lost all that he had; his house fell; would that were all! it crushed his sons also. And, to see that patience had great place in him, hear what he answered; "The Lord gave, the Lord hath taken away; as it pleased the Lord, so hath it been done; blessed be the name of the Lord." He hath taken what He gave, is He lost Who gave? He hath taken what He gave. As if he should say, He hath taken away all, let Him take all, send me away naked, and let me keep Him. What shall I lack if I have God? or what is the good of all else to me, if I have not God? Then it came to his flesh, he was stricken with a wound from head to foot; he was one running sore, one mass of crawling worms: and showed himself immovable in his God, stood fixed. The woman wanted, devil's helper as she was not husband's comforter, to put him up to blaspheme God. "How long," said she, "dost thou suffer" so and so; "speak some word against the Lord, and die." So then, because he had been brought low, he was to be exalted. And this the Lord did, in order to show it to men; as for His servant, He kept greater things for him in heaven. So then Job who was brought low, He exalted; the devil who was lifted up, He brought low: for "He puts down one and sets up another." But let not any man, my beloved brethren, when he suffers any such-like tribulations, look for a reward here: for instance, if he suffer any losses, let him not peradventure say, "The Lord gave, the Lord hath taken away; as it pleased the Lord, so is it done: blessed be the name of the Lord;" only with the mind to receive twice as much again. Let patience praise God, not avarice. If what thou hast lost thou seeks to receive back twofold, and therefore praises God, it is of covetousness thou praises, not of love. Do not imagine this to be the example of that holy man; thou deceives thyself. When Job was enduring all, he was not hoping for to have twice as much again. Both in his first confession when he bore up under his losses, and bore out to the grave the dead bodies of his sons, and in the second when he was now suffering torments of sores in his flesh, ye may observe what I am saying. Of his former confession the words run thus: "The Lord gave, and the Lord hath taken away: as it pleased the Lord, so is it done: blessed be the name of the Lord." He might have said, "The Lord gave, and the Lord hath taken away; He that took away can once more give; can bring back more than He took." He said not this, but, "As it pleased the Lord," said he, "so is it done:" because it pleases Him, let it please me: let not that which hath pleased the good Lord misplease His submissive servant; what pleased the Physician, not misplease the sick man.

Hear his other confession: "Thou hast spoken," said he to his wife, "like one of the foolish women. If we have received good at the hand of the Lord, why shall we not bear evil?" He did not add, what, if he had said it, would have been true. "The Lord is able both to bring back my flesh into its former condition, and that which He hath taken away from us, to make manifold more:" lest he should seem to have endured in hope of this. This was not what he said, not what he hoped. But, that we might be taught, did the Lord that for him, not hoping for it, by which we should be taught, that God was with him: because if He had not also restored to him those things, there was the crown indeed, but hidden, and we could not see it. And therefore what says the divine Scripture in exhorting to patience and hope of things future, not reward of things present? "Ye have heard of the patience of Job, and have seen the end of the Lord." Why is it, "the patience of Job," and not, Ye have seen the end of Job himself? Thou would open thy mouth for the "twice as much;" would say, "Thanks be to God; let me bear up: I receive twice as much again, like Job." "Patience of Job, end of the Lord." The patience of Job we know, and the end of the Lord we know. What end of the Lord? "My God, my God, why hast Thou forsaken Me?" They are the words of the Lord hanging on the cross. He did as it were leave Him for present felicity, not leave Him for eternal immortality. In this is "the end of the Lord." The Jews hold Him, the Jews insult, the Jews bind Him, crown Him with thorns, dishonor Him with spitting, scourge Him, overwhelm Him with reviling, hang Him upon the tree, pierce Him with a spear, last of all bury Him. He was as it were left: but by whom? By those insulting ones. Therefore thou shall but to this end have patience, that thou mayest rise again and not die, that is, never die, even as Christ. For so we read, "Christ rising from the dead henceforth dies not."

11. "He ascended into heaven:" believe. "He sits at the right hand of the Father:" believe. By sitting, understand dwelling: as [in Latin] we say of any person, "In that country he dwelt (sedit) three years." The Scripture also has that expression, that such a one dwelt (sedisse) in a city for such a time. Not meaning that he sat and never rose up? On this account the dwellings of men are called seats (sedes). Where people are seated (in this sense), are they always sitting? Is there no rising, no walking, no lying down? And yet they are called seats (sedes). In this way, then, believe an inhabiting of Christ on the right hand of God the Father: He is there. And let not your heart say to you, What is He doing? Do not want to seek what is not permitted to find: He is there; it suffices you. He is blessed, and from blessedness which is called the right hand of the Father, of very blessedness the name is, right hand of the Father. For if we shall take it carnally, then because He sits on the right hand of the Father, the Father will be on His left hand. Is it consistent with piety so to put Them together, the Son on the right, the Father on the left? There it is all right-hand, because no misery is there.

12. "Thence He shall come to judge the quick and dead." The quick, who shall be alive and remain; the dead, who shall have gone before. It may also be understood thus: The living, the just; the dead, the unjust. For He judges both, rendering unto each his own. To the just He will say in the judgment, "Come, ye blessed of

My Father, receive the kingdom prepared for you from the beginning of the world. "For this prepare yourselves, for these things hope, for this live, and so live, for this believe, for this be baptized, that it may be said to you, "Come ye blessed of My Father, receive the kingdom prepared for you from the foundation of the world." To them on the left hand, what? "Go into everlasting fire prepared for the devil and his angels." Thus will they be judged by Christ, the quick and the dead. We have spoken of Christ's first nativity, which is without time; spoken of the other in the fullness of time, Christ's nativity of the Virgin; spoken of the passion of Christ; spoken of the coming of Christ to judgment. The whole is spoken, that was to be spoken of Christ, God's Only Son, our Lord. But not yet is the Trinity perfect.

13. It follows in the Creed, "And in the Holy Ghost." This Trinity, one God, one nature, one substance, one power; highest equality, no division, no diversity, perpetual dearness of love. Would ye know the Holy Ghost, that He is God? Be baptized, and ye will be His temple. The Apostle says, "Know ye not that your bodies are the temple within you of the Holy Ghost, Whom ye have of God?" A temple is for God: thus also Solomon, king and prophet, was bidden to build a temple for God. If he had built a temple for the sun or moon or some star or some angel, would not God condemn him? Because therefore he built a temple for God he showed that he worshipped God. And of what did he build? Of wood and stone, because God deigned to make unto Himself by His servant a house on earth, where He might be asked, where He might be had in mind. Of which blessed Stephen says, "Solomon built Him a house; howbeit the Most High

dwelleth not in temples made by hand." If then our bodies are the temple of the Holy Ghost, what manner of God is it that built a temple for the Holy Ghost? But it was God. For if our bodies be a temple of the Holy Ghost, the same built this temple for the Holy Ghost, that built our bodies. Listen to the Apostle saying, "God hath tempered the body, giving unto that which lacked the greater honor;" when he was speaking of the different members that there should be no schisms in the body. God created our body. The grass, God created; our body Who created? How do we prove that the grass is God's creating? He that clothes, the same creates. Read the Gospel, "If then the grass of the fields," says it, "which to-day is, and to-morrow is cast into the oven, God so clothed." He, then, creates Who clothes. And the Apostle: "Thou fool, that which thou sows is not quickened except it die; and that which thou sows, thou sows not that body that shall be, but a bare grain, as perchance of wheat, or of some other corn; but God giveth it a body as He would, and to each one of seeds its proper body." If then it be God that builds our bodies, God that builds our members, and our bodies are the temple of the Holy Ghost, doubt not that the Holy Ghost is God. And do not add as it were a third God; because Father and Son and Holy Ghost is One God. So believe ye.

14. It follows after commendation of the Trinity, "The Holy Church." God is pointed out, and His temple. "For the temple of God is holy," says the Apostle, "which (temple) are ye." This same is the holy Church, the one Church, the true Church, the catholic Church, fighting against all heresies: fight, it can: be fought down, it cannot. As for heresies, they went all out of it, like as

unprofitable branches pruned from the vine: but itself abides in its root, in its Vine, in its charity. "The gates of hell shall not prevail against it."

15. "Forgiveness of sins." Ye have [this article of] the Creed perfectly in you when ye receive Baptism. Let none say, "I have done this or that sin: perchance that is not forgiven me." What hast thou done? How great a sin hast thou done? Name any heinous thing thou hast committed, heavy, horrible, which thou shudders even to think of: have done what thou wilt: hast thou killed Christ? There is not than that deed any worse, because also than Christ there is nothing better. What a dreadful thing is it to kill Christ! Yet the Jews killed Him, and many afterwards believed on Him and drank His blood: they are forgiven the sin which they committed. When ye have been baptized, hold fast a good life in the commandments of God, that ye may guard your Baptism even unto the end. I do not tell you that ye will live here without sin; but they are venial, without which this life is not. For the sake of all sins was Baptism provided; for the sake of light sins, without which we cannot be, was prayer provided. What hath the Prayer? "Forgive us our debts, as we also forgive our debtors." Once for all we have washing in Baptism, every day we have washing in prayer. Only, do not commit those things for which ye must needs be separated from Christ's body: which be far from you! For those whom ye have seen doing penance, have committed heinous things, either adulteries or some enormous crimes: for these they do penance. Because if theirs had been light sins, to blot out these daily prayer would suffice.

16. In three ways then are sins remitted in the Church; by Baptism, by prayer, by the greater humility of penance; yet God doth not remit sins but to the baptized. The very sins which He remits first, He remits not but to the baptized. When? when they are baptized. The sins which are after remitted upon prayer, upon penance, to whom He remits, it is to the baptized that He remitted. For how can they say, "Our Father," who are not yet born sons? The Catechumens, so long as they be such, have upon them all their sins. If Catechumens, how much more Pagans? how much more heretics? But to heretics we do not change their baptism. Why? because they have baptism in the same way as a deserter has the soldier's mark: just so these also have Baptism; they have it, but to be condemned thereby, not crowned. And yet if the deserter himself, being amended, begin to do duty as a soldier, does any man dare to change his mark?

17. We believe also "the resurrection of the flesh," which went before in Christ: that the body too may have hope of that which went before in its Head. The Head of the Church, Christ: the Church, the body of Christ. Our Head is risen, ascended into heaven: where the Head, there also the members. In what way the resurrection of the flesh? Lest any should chance to think it like as Lazarus's resurrection, that thou mayest know it to be not so, it is added, "Into life everlasting." God regenerate you! God preserve and keep you! God bring you safe unto Himself, Who is the Life Everlasting. Amen.

On the Creed

www.ingramcontent.com/pod-product-compliance
Lightning Source LLC
Chambersburg PA
CBHW052046070526
44584CB00018B/2639